The 23rd Psalm

The Lord is my shepherd;

I shall not want.

He maketh me to lie down in green pastures:

He leadeth me beside the still waters.

He restoreth my soul:

He leadeth me in the paths of righteousness for his name's sake.

Yea, though I walk through the valley of the shadow of death,

I will fear no evil.

For thou art with me; thy rod and thy staff they comfort me.

Thou preparest a table before me in the presence of mine enemies:

Thou anointest my head with oil; my cup runneth over.

Surely goodness and mercy shall follow me all the days of my life:

And I will dwell in the house of the Lord for ever.

This beautifully illustrated edition of the 23rd Psalm presents a sensitive combination of words and pictures to help children to a greater appreciation and understanding of this well-loved expression of faith.

LADYBIRD BOOKS, INC.
Auburn, Maine 04210 U.S.A.
© LADYBIRD BOOKS LTD 1989
Loughborough, Leicestershire, England

Printed in England

The Lord Is My Shepherd

Illustrated by LYNNE WILLEY

Ladybird Books

The Lord
is my
shepherd;

I shall
not want.

He maketh me
to lie down
in green
pastures:

He leadeth me
beside the
still waters.

He restoreth
my soul:

He leadeth me in the paths of righteousness for his name's sake.

Yea, though I walk
through the
valley of the shadow
of death, I will fear
no evil.

For thou
art with me;
thy rod and thy staff
they comfort me.

Thou preparest
a table before me
in the presence of
mine enemies:

Thou anointest
my head with oil;
my cup
runneth over.

*Surely
goodness and mercy
shall follow me
all the days
of my life:*

*And I will
dwell in the house
of the Lord
for ever.*